DOWNLOAD YOUR FREE INTERACTIVE DIGITAL GUIDE!

This entire guide is available as an interactive digital pdf and it's FREE with your purchase of this print version.

Use the QR code below and enter

BIGISLANDWITHKIDSDD

as the coupon code at check out.

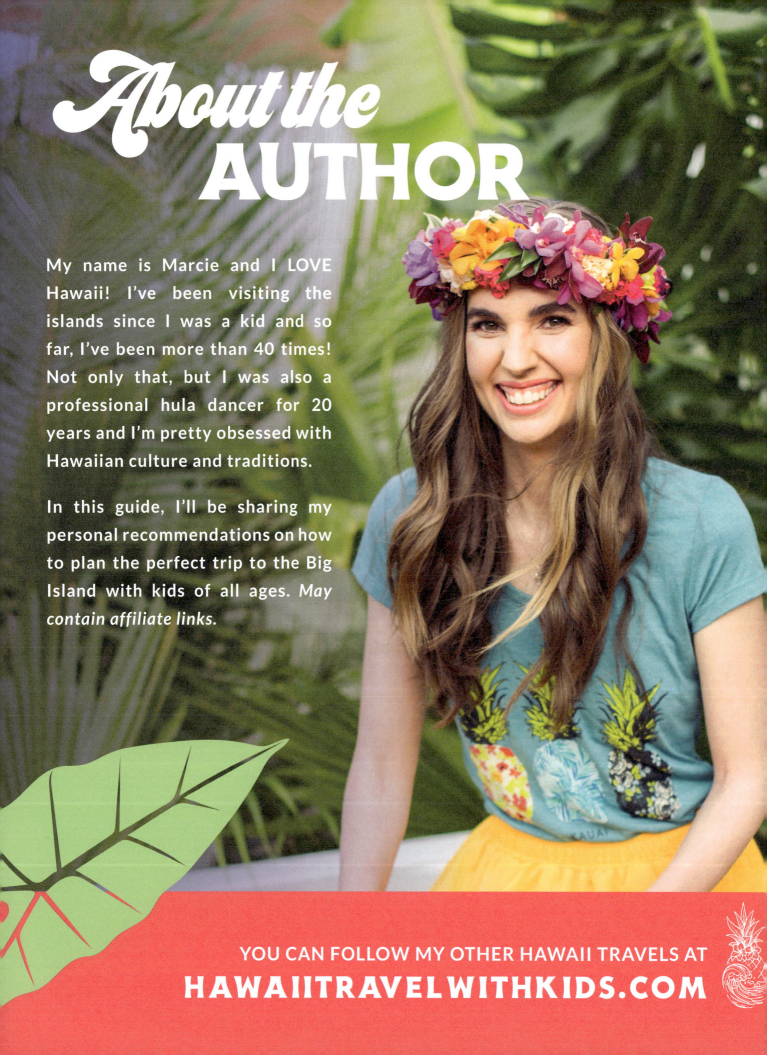

About the
AUTHOR

My name is Marcie and I LOVE Hawaii! I've been visiting the islands since I was a kid and so far, I've been more than 40 times! Not only that, but I was also a professional hula dancer for 20 years and I'm pretty obsessed with Hawaiian culture and traditions.

In this guide, I'll be sharing my personal recommendations on how to plan the perfect trip to the Big Island with kids of all ages. *May contain affiliate links.*

YOU CAN FOLLOW MY OTHER HAWAII TRAVELS AT
HAWAIITRAVELWITHKIDS.COM

ISLAND *overview*

The Big Island is one of the best places for an adventurous trip to Hawaii. It's the largest Hawaiian island, and also the newest. This is one of the best islands for people who want to go hiking, snorkel with Manta Rays, see impressive waterfalls, and explore Hawaii Volcanoes National Park.

While most people choose to stay in Kona (on the Westside), there are lots of amazing things to do all over the island.

10 things to know
BEFORE YOUR TRIP

 LOOK FOR DIRECT FLIGHTS

If you are flying to Hawaii from the Mainland, there are tons of direct flights to Kona from the West Coast. Usually, people fly to Honolulu and then take an inter-island flight to Kona. This flight is usually about 45 minutes long and can cost around $120. So, your best bet is to fly directly into Kona to save both time and money on your Big Island Hawaii vacation.

 YOU WILL NEED A RENTAL CAR

No matter where you stay on the Big Island (or any island), you're going to want to rent a car in Hawaii. That's because some of the best things to do in Kona require driving and the Big Island doesn't have great public transportation. And you won't find as many tour companies that will pick you up at your resort (unlike Waikiki). As far as Big Island car rentals, the cheapest place I've found is Discount Hawaii Car Rental. They get the best rates from top national companies like Alamo, Dollar, Thrifty, Avis, Enterprise, Budget, and Payless. Check out the latest prices and more details.

 **CHECK TO SEE IF VOLCANOES ARE ACTIVE**

Whenever people are disappointed about their Big Island trip, it's usually because they didn't see any lava. And it's not for lack of trying. They always go to Hawaii Volcanoes National Park, where there are 2 volcanoes. However, they don't take the time to check to see if the volcanoes are active before they go. It's really important to set realistic expectations before you explore Hawaii Volcanoes National Park.

 HAWAII VOLCANOES NATIONAL PARK IS A FULL DAY TRIP

Whether or not the volcanoes are active, there are still plenty of things to do at Hawaii Volcanoes National Park. And I'm serious when I say it will take all day. If you're staying in Kona, it's going to take about 2.5 hours to drive to Hawaii Volcanoes National Park. You'll also want to factor in the same time to get back to your Big Island hotel. Once you're there, head to the Visitor's Center and see what kinds of events and ranger programs are happening. Then, you might want to go hiking, explore lava tubes, check out the crater, or do a scenic drive through the park.

 MOST BIG ISLAND RESORTS ARE IN KONA

When visiting the Big Island, you might be wondering if you should stay in Hilo or Kona. Most of the Big Island hotels are located in Kona. And that's where you'll find some of the fancier resorts, as well. Hilo is more laid back and you'll probably need to stay in a VRBO or Hawaii vacation rental home. Kona is definitely the more touristy side of the island, so there are lots of luaus, restaurants, and activities.

BIG ISLAND HOTELS

6 SPLIT YOUR STAY BETWEEN KONA AND HILO

If you really want to explore the Big Island, it makes the most sense to do a split stay. That's because Hilo and Kona are about 3 hours away from each other. And that's a lot of driving if you want to explore the South, East, or North Shore of the Big Island. Kona is where you'll take advantage of Big Island activities and attractions. Plus, enjoy the resort experience. Then, you can head to Hilo where you can do Hawaii Volcanoes National Park, explore Big Island waterfalls, go hiking, and more.

7 AVOID MERRIE MONARCH WEEK

One of the biggest events in Hawaii is the Merrie Monarch Festival. It happens every year in April on the Big Island. The festival brings in large hula dance troupes from all over the world and attracts lots of festival attendees. Because of this, flights and hotel rooms are hard to find (and expensive). Plus, the Big Island gets very crowded. So, unless you are planning on attending the festival, avoid visiting the Big Island that week.

8 VISIT A KONA COFFEE PLANTATION

One of the things Hawaii is known for is coffee and the most famous one is Kona Coffee. It's also one of the priciest. If you're wondering why it's so expensive, you should head to a coffee farm in Kona to find out exactly what makes up the tasty coffee of Kona. Most tours offer education about the coffee industry, its culture, history, and processes that play an integral role in creating your favorite cup of java. Plus, you will get to pick up quite a number of Kona coffee beans from the farms on your tour.

BEST KONA COFFEE FARMS ⊘

9 GO NIGHT DIVING WITH MANTA RAYS

One of the top things to do on the Big Island is snorkel or dive with Manta Rays at night. These majestic creatures are huge and their wingspan is close to 29 feet! You won't want to miss your opportunity to see them up close. The best way to do this is by joining a Manta Ray boat tour from Kona. You'll hop on at dusk and as soon as it's dark, they will turn on floodlights that will attract plankton, which will attract the Manta Rays. Then, you'll hop into the water and hang onto large rafts and wait for the beautiful Manta Rays to make their appearance.

MANTA RAY BOAT TOUR

10 THERE ARE A LOT OF BIG ISLAND LUAUS

A lot of times, I hear people say that you only need to do a luau once because it's all the same. As a professional hula dancer, I can emphatically say that most Big Island luaus are special in their own way. One of the most popular Big Island luaus is the Hawaii Loa Luau at the Fairmont Orchid. It's in the Waikoloa area and has some of the best menu options and entertainment. There's also Haleo Luau, which celebrates the history of Keauhou and those who came from the area. Plus, they share the story of King Kamehameha's birth. And there are also Hawaii luaus that incorporate storytelling, theatrics, and lots of fire.

BEST BIG ISLAND LUAUS

BIG ISLAND *airports*

When booking your airfare to the Big Island, you'll either fly into the Ellison Onizuka Kona International Airport at Keahole (the most popular) or the Hilo International Airport. Both airports are incredibly small.

KONA AIRPORT

If you are flying into Kona, don't be surprised if you exit the airplane outside and walk over to their small baggage claim area. Since it can take a while before the bags come out, I like to use the restroom and then pick up brochures and tourist magazines so I can thumb through them later (they have lots of coupons inside). Once you have your luggage, follow the signs to the rental car shuttle bus.

For your flight home, you'll need to go through their agricultural inspection, so don't try to take home any fruit or plants. There are a couple of places to eat and a little gift shop for last-minute souvenirs.

HILO AIRPORT

If you are flying into Hilo, you'll disembark through jetways to the second level of the terminal. You may take an escalator, elevator, or stairs to get to the ground-level baggage claim area. Then follow the signs for rental cars.

For your flight home, you'll need to go through their agricultural inspection, so don't try to take home any fruit or plants. There are a couple of places to eat and a little gift shop for last-minute souvenirs.

WHERE TO STAY
with kids

There are four popular areas for families: Kailua-Kona, Waikoloa, Hilo, and Volcano. You'll find an array of beach resorts and vacation rentals on the Big Island in these four locations.

The trickiest thing about a Big Island vacation is that the island is HUGE and it can take a long time to drive places. So, the most important thing to think about when figuring out where to stay on the Big Island is your vacation itinerary.

- Are you planning on driving around the island for a few days?

- Do you have scheduled activities somewhere?

- Would you like to stay at a resort and just relax?

Answering these questions will help you determine the smartest place to stay.

Another thing to think about is whether or not you're looking for a resort with a kids club. The price varies based on the resort, time of year, and whether you want a half-day or full day. We have spent between $50-$60 for a half-day, but you'll want to check out the resort for details.

Continued on the next page

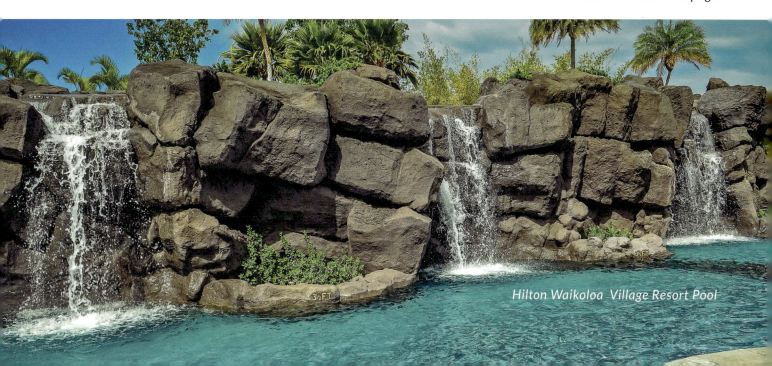

Hilton Waikoloa Village Resort Pool

KAILUA-KONA
West Shore

For families traveling with small children, I usually suggest they stay in Kailua-Kona because it's the main hub on the Big Island. This is where you'll find the most resorts and vacation rentals at all price points. Plus, it's close to a lot of activities and attractions. The most desirable area is along Ali'i Drive.

Splurge

COURTYARD BY MARRIOTT KING KAMEHAMEHA'S KONA BEACH HOTEL

The Courtyard by Marriott King Kamehameha's Kona Beach Hotel is the perfect place for families looking for a small lagoon, infinity pool, on-site activities, a luau, a spa, and dining options. It's in a great location for walking along Ali'i Drive to visit shops and restaurants.

PRICES & DETAILS ⊙

ROYAL KONA RESORT

The Royal Kona Resort is a moderately-priced hotel with a private lagoon, pool area with a kids pool, a luau, laundry, and dining options. It's also on Ali'i Drive and across the street from an ABC store.

PRICES & DETAILS ⊙

Save

KONA SEASIDE HOTEL

The Kona Seaside Hotel is a great option for budget travelers. They have an outdoor pool, views of Kailua Pier, and no resort fees.

PRICES & DETAILS ⊙

WAIKOLOA

Another popular resort area for families is Waikoloa. This is north of the Kona airport and it's fairly remote, so it's ideal for people who want a resort vacation with a few day trips.

Splurge

HILTON WAIKOLOA VILLAGE

Many families choose to stay at the Hilton Waikoloa Village because they have a ton of kid-friendly activities like swimming with dolphins, an on-site luau, children's programming, a massive pool area, and lots of shops and restaurants. They even have a monorail and boats to take you to different areas of the massive resort.

PRICES & DETAILS ⊙

FAIRMONT ORCHID

The Fairmont Orchid is another great option with a gorgeous white sand beach, pools, a spa, an on-site luau, kids' activities, and several restaurants.

PRICES & DETAILS ⊙

Save

KINGS' LAND

Kings' Land is actually more of a moderately-priced hotel than a budget hotel, but it's affordable compared to the other resorts in Waikoloa. These suites offer full kitchens, washer/dryers, and a shuttle to places within the Waikoloa Beach Resort.

PRICES & DETAILS ⊙

HILO

If you'll be spending time on the East shore of the Big Island to see waterfalls, Waipio Valley, and want to day trip to Hawaii Volcanoes National Park, it can make sense to spend a few nights in Hilo. Accommodations are MUCH cheaper on this side of the island.

Splurge

GRAND NANILOA HOTEL

The Grand Naniloa Hotel is one of my favorite Hilo hotels. It has gorgeous sunrise views over Hilo Bay. Plus they have an on-site restaurant, bar, a great gift shop with grab-and-go food, and free cookies when you arrive.

PRICES & DETAILS ⊖

CASTLE HILO HAWAIIAN HOTEL

Another option is the Castle Hilo Hawaiian Hotel right next to Liliuokalani Gardens. They have an on-site steakhouse.

PRICES & DETAILS ⊖

Save

HILO REEDS BAY HOTEL

A good budget Hilo hotel is the Hilo Reeds Bay Hotel. It is a small hotel with laundry facilities.

PRICES & DETAILS ⊖

VOLCANO

VOLCANO HOUSE

If you really want to take your time exploring Hawaii Volcanoes National Park, I highly recommend spending the night at Volcano House. It's the only hotel located inside the park and it's easy to walk to many of the top attractions. Plus, if the volcano is erupting, you can see the glow from your room!

PRICES & DETAILS ⊖

THINGS TO SEE

1 PU'UHONUA O HŌNAUNAU NATIONAL HISTORICAL PARK ⊙

This is an incredible national park where you can see replica tiki statues and structures. **Download the NPS app** to learn more about the history of this "Place of Refuge" and why it was so important in ancient Hawaii.

2 PAINTED CHURCH ⊙

This is a quick stop but totally worth the drive. It's an impressive little church where the entire interior has brightly colored paintings on the wall and ceiling. It's stunning!

3 KALOKO-HONOKŌHAU NATIONAL HISTORICAL PARK ⊙

This park is actually split into a few different sections. There's the beach area (where you can see sea turtles and an ancient Hawaiian structure), the fishing ponds, and the visitor's center (that has an awesome interpretive walk).

Hilo

1 AKAKA FALLS

One of the most beautiful Big Island waterfalls is Akaka Falls, just outside of Hilo. There's a really easy, paved walking trail to the scenic lookout. It's a great stop as you drive along the coast.

2 WAIPIO VALLEY

If you want a glimpse at Old Hawaii, head down to Waipio Valley. The only way to do this is to either hike down or catch the Waipio Valley Shuttle (which is what I recommend).

GET TICKETS HERE ⊙

3 HAWAII TROPICAL BIORESERVE & GARDEN ⊙

This is one of the prettiest botanical gardens in Hawaii. There's a well-kept path that takes you to a hidden waterfall, a giant tiki statue, a wishing well, a reflection pond, and you'll see so many tropical flowers.

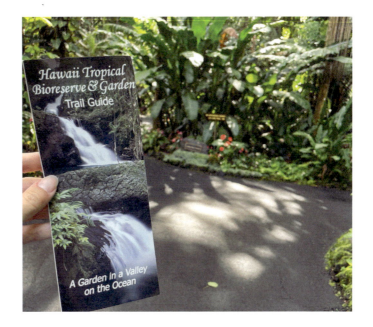

Hawaii Volcanoes National Park

1 THURSTON LAVA TUBE ⊙

One of the easiest hikes to do with kids is to explore the Thurston Lava Tube. It's a short hike that takes you through an actual lava tube. It's helpful to have flashlights or a headlamp.

2 SULPHUR BANKS ⊙

This is a nice walking path through the sulfur banks and you can learn about them through interpretive signs.

3 CHAIN OF CRATERS ⊙

This is a 19-mile drive that takes you from the top of the crater all the way down to ocean level. It's a gorgeous drive and there are places to pull over and see where lava once flowed.

KID FRIENDLY ACTIVITIES

Beaches

1 KAMAKAHONU BEACH ⊙
WHERE: KAILUA-KONA

Kamakahonu Beach (commonly called King Kam Beach) is one of the best kid-friendly beaches in Kona. It's situated right by the King Kamehameha hotel on the popular Ali'i Drive.

2 HAPUNA BEACH ⊙
WHERE: KOHALA

Another awesome beach on the Big Island for kids is Hapuna Beach in the South Kohala area. It's the longest white sand beach on the Island of Hawaii.

3 ONEKAHAKAHA BEACH PARK ⊙
WHERE: HILO

The best kid-friendly Hilo beach is Onekahakaha Beach Park. Here, you'll find a picnic pavilion, restrooms, and showers. And the water is protected by a lava rock seawall.

Hikes

1 KALAHUIPUA'A FISHPONDS TRAIL LOOP ⊙
WHERE: PUAKO

This is an easy 1.7-mile walking trail where you can explore a cave, walk across a lava field, look for petroglyphs, see fishponds created by early Hawaiians, and check out a tidepool.

2 LAVA TREE TRAIL ⊙
WHERE: PAHOA

If you want a toddler-friendly trail, this is only 0.7 miles long and perfect for little ones. It's a great place to see lava formations as well as wildflowers and even some birds.

3 AKAKA FALLS ⊙
WHERE: HILO

This is a super easy 0.5-mile paved loop trail that takes you to an awesome view of Akaka Falls. There's actually a shorter trail if you have little ones.

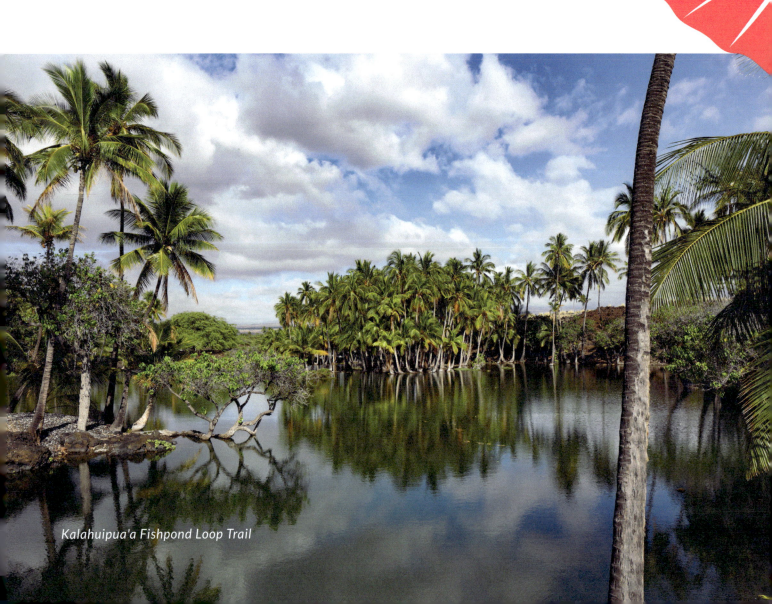
Kalahuipua'a Fishpond Loop Trail

Playgrounds

1 PANA'EWA RAINFOREST ZOO ⊙

WHERE: HILO

This is a free zoo that also has an incredible play area. They even have a small climbing area for toddlers adjacent to the playground. And there are picnic areas.

2 KAMAKANA PLAYGROUND ⊙

WHERE: NEAR KONA

This is a whimsical playground that features a large wooden castle, a canoe, a massive slide tire swings, a zipline, and a 22-foot long whale sculpture to climb on. There's even a separate area for little kids.

3 WAIMEA COMMUNITY PARK ⊙

WHERE: WAIMEA

If you're looking for a beautiful destination playground, head up to Waimea and check out this park. Here, you'll find swings, slides, monkey bars, bridges, things to climb, and things to spin on. It's also the ultimate hide-and-seek park.

Adventures

1 CULTURAL ATV TOUR ⊙
WHERE: KONA

Aloha Adventure Farms has both ATVs (for people ages 16+) as well as UTVs for kids ages 5-15. You go into the jungle and stop at several Polynesian villages for hands-on cultural activities. It's incredible! They also have a tiki wood carving workshop for kids ages 8 and older.

PRICES & DETAILS ⊙

2 KONA ATLANTIS SUBMARINE ⊙
WHERE: KONA

This is a great way to explore underwater without getting wet. You'll see sunken ships and tons of tropical fish on this narrated tour in Kona. Out of all three Atlantis submarine adventures in Hawaii, this one is hands-down our favorite!

PRICES & DETAILS ⊙

3 MANTA RAY NIGHT SNORKEL ⊙
WHERE: KONA

Kona is one of the few places in the world where you can swim with Manta Rays. This tour is open to kids of all ages. It's a once-in-a-lifetime experience.

PRICES & DETAILS ⊙

Tours

1 FRIENDS OF HAWAII VOLCANOES NATIONAL PARK TOUR

While you can explore Hawaii Volcanoes National Park on your own, you'll get a TON more out of the experience with a guided tour. This is a private tour led by docents who will tailor the itinerary based on your interests.

PRICES & DETAILS ⊙

2 VOLCANOES CIRCLE ISLAND TOUR

If you're staying in Kona but want to see the highlights across the Big Island, this guided tour takes you to Hawaii Volcanoes National Park, Waipio Valley, and several waterfalls. It's a great way to see the sights without being focused on driving.

PRICES & DETAILS ⊙

3 KONA COFFEE FARM TOUR

There are tons of Kona Coffee farms you can explore. One of the best farms to visit is Heavenly Hawaiian Coffee Farm. They have a variety of tours for all interest levels. Plus lots of coffee tastings.

PRICES & DETAILS ⊙

Luaus

 HAWAII LOA LUAU
WHERE: WAIKOLOA

This is one of the best luaus in Waikoloa and it takes place at the Fairmont Orchid Resort. They have an extensive luau buffet including a poke station and a carving station for their roasted pig. The entertainment here is also pretty amazing.

PRICES & DETAILS ⊙

VOYAGERS OF THE PACIFIC LUAU
WHERE: KONA

This is a great luau with Polynesian dancing and amazing sunset views at the Royal Kona Resort. They also have some of the BEST luau food I've ever had.

FIND BEST PRICES

LEGENDS OF HAWAII LUAU
WHERE: WAIKOLOA

If you're staying at the Hilton Waikoloa Village (or anywhere in Waikoloa) this is a great luau for kids. They have a bunch of children's activities as well as unlimited drinks for grown-ups. It's also located right in front of the ocean with beautiful sunset views.

PRICES & DETAILS ⊙

BEST DINING OPTIONS

FAST CASUAL RESTAURANTS

1 KA'ALOA'S SUPER J'S
WHERE: CAPTAIN COOK

If you're looking for authentic Hawaiian food, you'll definitely want to hit up Ka'aloa's Super J's in Captain Cook. They specialize in chicken and pork lau lau (meat steamed in taro leaves) as well as traditional kalua pork.

2 KEN'S HOUSE OF PANCAKES
WHERE: HILO

This is a Hilo institution. It's a retro diner with classic American dishes as well as local favorites like saimin and teriyaki beef. They offer kid sizes for many of their menu items.

3 TEX DRIVE IN
WHERE: HONOKA'A

If you're driving up the Honoka'a Coast, make sure to stop by Tex Drive In in Honoka'a. They are most famous for their malasadas (which are super cheap). But, they also have a great drive in menu with items like loco moco, burgers, fries, hot dogs, Hawaiian food, and so much more.

FOOD TRUCKS

1 ISLAND STYLE GRINDZ
WHERE: WAIMEA, HAWI, KONA, HILO, AND OTHER HAWAII ISLAND TOWN

This is THE place to go if you want an authentic Hawaiian plate lunch. You'll need to head to their <u>Instagram</u> page in order to find out where they'll be and the hours each day.

2 JOHNNY'S MAKANI
WHERE: KAILUA-KONA

Whether or not you stop to play golf at Makani Golf Course, you'll definitely want to hit up this food truck. They have burgers, sandwiches, and fries.

3 MANUELA MALASADA
WHERE: KAILUA-KONA

This is a famous malasada food truck that was featured on HGTV. You'll definitely want to get their malasadas, which are like giant donut holes with sugar on them.

SHAVE ICE

1 GECKO GIRLZ SHAVE ICE
WHERE: KONA

One of the best places to get shave ice in Kona is Gecko Girlz. It's a walk-up counter right off Ali'i Drive. They have a pretty extensive menu including ice cream at the bottom and even getting it snowcapped (drizzled in condensed milk).

2 SCANDINAVIAN SHAVE ICE
WHERE: KONA

If you're heading to Hulihee Palace, you'll definitely want to plan a stop here. Scandi's has been voted the best shave ice in Hawaii for good reason. They have 65 different flavors to choose from and you can get ice cream or frozen yogurt at the bottom.

3 ULULANI'S SHAVE ICE
WHERE: KONA

This iconic Maui shave ice company has a location at the King Kamehameha Hotel in Kona. They have some of the tastiest shave ice in Hawaii made with real fruit syrups. This is a must-stop place.

KID-FRIENDLY SIT DOWN RESTAURANTS

① HUGGO'S ON THE ROCKS ⊙
WHERE: KONA

This is the beachfront cafe right next to Huggo's (which I'll talk about later). They have a full kids menu and lots of tasty non-alcoholic drinks for little ones. They even have live music and hula dancing on some evenings.

② LAVA LAVA BEACH CLUB ⊙
WHERE: WAIKOLOA

This is a sister restaurant to Huggo's on the Rocks. What's really cool about this place is that they have lawn games that are perfect to keep kids occupied while waiting for their food. Plus, they often have live Hawaiian music.

③ KONA BREWING COMPANY ⊙
WHERE: KONA

If you're looking for a place to eat in Kona with kids, head to the Kona Brewing Company. It's a fun restaurant with an array of locally made beer for grown-ups and an awesome kids menu with the food they will actually eat!

DATE NIGHT

① HUGGO'S ⊙
WHERE: KONA

This is the more upscale version of Huggo's on the Rocks. The views are epic and the food is incredible. They often have live Hawaiian music. It's right on Ali'i Drive so it's perfect for an after-dinner stroll.

② MERRIMAN'S BIG ISLAND ⊙
WHERE: WAIMEA

This is a top Hawaii restaurant chain that is perfect for a date night. The food is delicious and Merriman's is home to the BEST mai tai in Hawaii (it comes with lilikoi foam on top)!

③ NAPUA ⊙
WHERE: WAIKOLOA

This is an upscale Big Island restaurant that specializes in seafood and steak dishes. They do offer a kids menu if you end up needing to bring them along.

Family PHOTO SHOOT

One of our favorite things to do on the Big Island is a family photoshoot. I'm serious. The whole family gets a kick out of them and it usually ends up being a fun activity.

We set aside a few hours to get the whole family cleaned up and "camera ready." Then, we go to a pretty location with our photographer who makes us feel like total celebrities.

It really takes the pressure off taking "nice" family photos throughout the trip. And we usually print them to put on our wall, use them for holiday card photos, use them as the background on our phones, add to our photo books, and share them on social media.

It's really easy to set up a photoshoot on the Big Island. We like using **Flytographer**, which is a concierge photography website. You just type in that you're looking for photographers on the Big Island and it will show you several to choose from. You can take a look at their portfolios and pick the one you like best. Then, the concierge will sort out all the details. It's one of the most affordable ways to get professional photos on the Big Island. We've even gotten our photos back before the end of our trip, which is pretty amazing service.

RATES & AVAILABILITY (>)

Sample
ITINERARIES

Here are some Big Island itineraries to get you started on your trip. Keep in mind that if you have younger kids, you might just want to plan on morning activities and then go back to your hotel for afternoon naps or pool time. This itinerary starts in Kona and ends in Hilo.

DOWNLOAD MY BIG ISLAND MAP

Day 1  (Moderately Paced)

MORNING (6 HOURS)

BREAKFAST AT KONA COFFEE AND TEA

If you are flying to Kona from the Mainland, chances are that you will wake up much earlier than usual. Let's take advantage of that! Head over to Kona Coffee and Tea for some authentic Kona coffee and easy breakfast items. You can either enjoy it there or take it to go.

KONA COFFEE AND TEA ⊙

ALOHA ADVENTURE FARMS CULTURAL ATV TOUR

After enjoying breakfast, it's time to head to **Aloha Adventure Farms** to do their 2-hour cultural ATV tour. Since you'll need to wear long pants, I recommend booking the first tour of the morning so you can explore before it gets too hot. You can also add on the tiki wood carving workshop, if you like.

BOOK HERE ⊙

LUNCH AT KA'ALOA'S SUPER J'S

By now, you've probably worked up an appetite. Luckily, there's a really authentic Hawaiian restaurant that most tourists don't know about. It's called **Ka'aloa's Super J's** and they are famous for their lau lau and kalua pork. You can either eat there or take your food to go.

AFTERNOON (2 HOURS)

SWIM AND/OR RELAX AT YOUR HOTEL OR A BEACH

Since this was an action-packed morning with an early start, plan on spending the rest of your day swimming at your hotel pool or heading to a beach. Or, just relax/nap in your hotel room and soak in the air conditioning.

EVENING (2 HOURS)

DINNER ALONG ALI'I DRIVE

Since you had an early morning, find a restaurant along Ali'i Drive and have an early evening. Because of the time difference, you'll probably be hungry for dinner a bit earlier than usual. After dinner, grab shave ice or go souvenir shopping.

Day 2 *(Moderately Paced)*

MORNING (5 HOURS)

KALOKO-HONOKŌHAU NATIONAL HISTORIC PARK

Today, you'll be exploring the Kona Coast and Waimea Town. Your first stop will be Kaloko-Honokōhau National Historic Park. Head straight for the visitor's center to get a map and Junior Ranger booklet. Do the interpretive walk and then drive over to the marina. After you park, you'll do the short walk to get to Honokohau Beach. Here, you'll keep an eye out of Hawaiian Green Sea Turtles as you explore the ʻAiʻōpio fishtrap and Puʻuoina Heiau. Hop in your car to visit Kaloko Fishpond and then head back to the visitor's center to receive the Junior Ranger badge.

KALOKO-HONOKŌHAU NATIONAL HISTORIC PARK

AFTERNOON (3 HOURS)

WAIMEA TOWN

Next, you'll make your way up to Waimea town. This is where you'll see authentic Hawaiian cowboy country. You'll see lots of ranches and get a very different view of Hawaii. Stop in Waimea town to enjoy lunch. **Merriman's Big Island** is perfect for a nice, sit-down lunch. Or enjoy a casual meal at **The Fish and the Hog** or **Hawaiian Style Cafe**.

WAIMEA COMMUNITY PARK

After lunch, head to Waimea Community Park to let your kids get some wiggles out. This is a destination playground. Since the weather is a bit cooler up here, you might want to bring a light sweatshirt.

WAIMEA COMMUNITY PARK

EVENING (2 HOURS)

FAMILY PHOTO SHOOT

You'll end your fun-filled day with a family photo shoot in Kona during golden hour. Since it's on the west shore, there are plenty of places for epic sunset photos. Our favorite spot is Old Kona Airport Beach because of the variety of scenery. I really like working with **Flytographer** because they are really flexible and affordable. And you'll get your photos back within 5 days. That means you can post your photos on social media while you're still in Hawaii!

BOOK HERE ⊙

Day 3 (Moderately Paced)

MORNING (3 HOURS)

KONA ATLANTIS SUBMARINE RIDE

Head over to the Courtyard by Marriott King Kamehameha's Kona Beach Hotel and park your car. Walk to Kona Wave Cafe to get coffee and acai bowls to enjoy by the beach. When you're done, head inside the hotel to check in for your Kona Atlantis Submarine ride. First, you'll head out on a little boat ride that features amazing views of Kailua Bay and the Kona coastline. Then, you'll climb down into a passenger submarine that will take you 100 feet below the surface. It's a great opportunity to see some shipwrecks. Plus, you never know what types of fish and sea life will make a surprise appearance.

BOOK HERE ⊙

AFTERNOON (4 HOURS)

KING KAM BEACH

After exploring under the water, it's time to hang out above surface. Since you're already parked at the hotel, you might as well take advantage of playing at King Kam Beach. It's a really tiny lagoon area that's perfect for little ones. There are restrooms nearby to change into swimsuits. Plus, you can enjoy lunch there and even get Ululani's Shave Ice.

KING KAM BEACH ⊙

EVENING (2 HOURS)

LUAU OR SWIMMING WITH MANTA RAYS

You have two options for evening activities tonight: attend a luau or swim with Manta Rays. If you're heading to another island, save the luau to do there and opt for night swimming with Manta Rays since it's a unique opportunity.

BOOK MANTA RAY EXPERIENCE ⊙

Day 4 *(Relaxed Paced)*

MORNING (4 HOURS)

DRIVE TO HAWAII VOLCANOES NATIONAL PARK

Today, you'll be packing up and heading to Hawaii Volcanoes National Park. The drive takes just under 2 hours with no stops. But, you'll definitely want to make some stops! I recommend downloading the Shaka Guide specifically for the drive from Kona to Hawaii Volcanoes National Park. It will give you a brief history of the areas as you drive past and offer additional stops along the drive.

DOWNLOAD SHAKA GUIDE

PUUHONUA O HONAUNAU NATIONAL HISTORIC PARK

Start with breakfast at **The Coffee Shack** in Captain Cook. The views are amazing and they have awesome coffee and food. Next, head to Puuhonua O Honaunau National Historic Park. You can pick up a Junior Ranger booklet and complete the tasks to earn a badge. You'll probably want about an hour to explore the area and take photos.

PUUHONUA O HONAUNAU NATIONAL HISTORIC PARK

ST. BENEDICT'S PAINTED CHURCH

Next, head to St. Benedict's Painted Church, which is just up the road. This is a really quick stop just to take some photos and spend a few minutes instead just soaking it all in. An optional stop is to get banana bread or fruit on Painted Church Road. There are lots of stands with a cash honor system.

ST. BENEDICT'S PAINTED CHURCH

AFTERNOON (3 HOURS)

KALAE

You'll continue your drive down to Kalae. This is the southern-most point in the United States. It's just cool to say you've been there. This is one of the best spots for cliff jumping on the Big Island. You can sit and watch brave people do it. Or if you have teens that are good swimmers, they might want to try themselves. An optional activity is to continue on to the Green Sand Beach. You aren't allowed to take a rental car there, so you'll need to pay a local to drive you there in a truck.

KALAE ⊙

LUNCH AT PUNALU'U BAKE SHOP

For lunch, head to **Punalu'u Bake Shop**. They are famous for their Hawaiian sweet bread. But, you can also pick up sandwiches and ice cream to enjoy in their large outdoor area.

EVENING (2 HOURS)

ARRIVE AT HAWAII VOLCANOES NATIONAL PARK

Your final stop is Hawaii Volcanoes National Park. You can make a quick stop at the visitor's center to pick up a Junior Ranger booklet, grab a park map, and to learn about the ranger programs for the next day. Then, check into **Volcano House** hotel (or a vacation rental home in Volcano). Enjoy dinner in Volcano or make a reservation to eat at **The Rim at Volcano House** for an epic view.

MAKE DINNER RESERVATIONS ⊙

HIKE TO SEE LAVA AT NIGHT

If your family still has energy (and the volcano is active), ask around for the best place to hike to see lava. You'll want to take flashlights and/or headlamps.

Day 5 (Fast Paced)

MORNING (5 HOURS)

HAWAII VOLCANOES NATIONAL PARK

You'll be spending the entire day exploring Hawaii Volcanoes National Park. This is a huge area so it's best to see it with a guide. Book a private 4-hour tour through Friends of Hawaii Volcanoes National Park. They will tailor the tour to your own interests and abilities. Definitely ask your tour guide for recommendations for what to do the rest of your day.

AFTERNOON (5 HOURS)

LUNCH AT VOLCANO HOUSE

After your tour, head to Volcano House for lunch. You can either make a reservation at The Rim, or eat at Uncle George's (they also have to-go sandwiches).

KILAUEA IKI TRAIL AND CHAIN OF CRATERS DRIVE

The rest of the afternoon will depend on what you saw/did on your tour. I recommend doing the Kilauea Iki Trail and enjoying the Chain of Craters drive. Another option is to talk with a park ranger to see what ranger programs they have going on during the day or recommendations to see lava.

EVENING (4 HOURS)

DRIVE TO HILO, CHECK-IN AND HAVE DINNER

Finally, you'll drive about 40 minutes to get to Hilo, where you'll spend the rest of your trip. Check into your hotel or vacation rental and then find somewhere for a hearty dinner. After all that exploring, your family will be a little tired and hungry.

Day 6 *(Moderately Paced)*

MORNING (5 HOURS)

HILO FARMERS MARKET AND RAINBOW FALLS

You'll start your morning by heading to the **Hilo Farmers Market** for breakfast and to try some new fruit. This is the most famous farmers market on the Big Island and it's fun for a quick stop. Then, you'll head up the street to Rainbow Falls (it's about a 5 minute drive). Park your car and walk a few steps for a super cute photo opportunity. There is ZERO hiking involved. This is a popular tourist attraction and it's easy to ask someone to take a family photo.

RAINBOW FALLS (>)

AKAKA FALLS STATE PARK

Next, you'll drive to Akaka Falls State Park. There is an entrance fee and a parking fee. Both of these go toward maintaining the trails. It's a really easy half-mile paved loop trail where you can see Akaka Falls. There's a shorter path you can take if you're pressed for time or want to conserve energy.

AKAKA FALLS STATE PARK (>)

HAWAII TROPICAL BIORESERVE & GARDEN

Your last stop of the morning will be Hawaii Tropical Bioreserve & Garden. This is a short, paved walking trail where you can see Onomea Waterfall, a huge tiki statue, a wishing well, lots of tropical flowers, and so much more.

HAWAII TROPICAL BIORESERVE & GARDEN (>)

AFTERNOON (3 HOURS)

LUNCH AT CAFE 100 AND FRESH MOCHI

For lunch, head back into Hilo and stop at **Cafe 100**. This is home to the original Loco Moco. They have an extensive menu that includes Hawaiian food as well as American diner food. Next, pick up fresh mochi from **Two Ladies Kitchen**. They are most famous for their fresh fruit stuffed mochi. You can order it ahead of time or stand in line.

HANG OUT AT YOUR HOTEL OR THE BEACH

Finally, head back to your hotel for pool time or relax at a local beach. After all the walking around to see waterfalls today, your kids will probably want to play in the water for a bit.

EVENING (2 HOURS)

Enjoy dinner near your hotel and rest up.

 **Day 7** *(Relaxed Paced)*

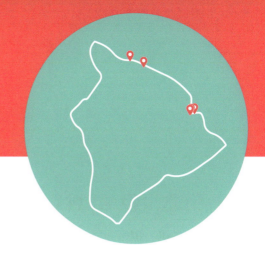

MORNING (3 HOURS)

WAIPIO VALLEY SHUTTLE TOUR

I saved the best for last for your final day on the Big Island of Hawaii. You'll be exploring one of the most beautiful and secluded places in Hawaii: Waipio Valley. The best way for families to visit Waipio Valley is by booking the Waipio Valley Shuttle Tour. You'll hop inside an open-window van that will take you past the Waipio Valley Lookout all the way down into the valley where you'll see wild horses, taro patches, and Hi'ilawe Falls. This is open to kids of all ages.

 **BOOK HERE** ⊙

ALTERNATIVE OPTION:
WAIPIO VALLEY HORSEBACK RIDING TOUR

If you are traveling with kids who are at least 7 years old, you can opt to do the Waipio Valley Horseback Riding Tour instead. You'll see all the same sights but get to explore the area a lot longer and really soak up the spectacular views.

 **BOOK HERE** ⊙

AFTERNOON (3 HOURS)

LUNCH AND SHOPPING

When you are finished touring Waipio Valley, grab lunch at Tex Drive In. This is an old-school drive in where you can get amazing local Hawaiian food or diner classics like hamburgers, hot dogs, and french fries. But, they are most famous for their malasadas. You'll definitely want to grab a bag of malasadas to enjoy back at your hotel or for breakfast before your flight home.

If you still have energy, park in Honoka'a town and peruse the little shops to find unique Big Island souvenirs.

EVENING (3 HOURS)

DINNER IN HILO

Enjoy one final meal in Hilo. A few top restaurant picks include Hilo Bay Cafe, Cafe Pesto, or Moon and Turtle.

TOP QUESTIONS
parents have about the Big Island

DO I NEED TO RENT A CAR?

Absolutely. It's really difficult to get around the Big Island without a car if you really want to explore the island. This is especially true if you have kids that need to be in car seats. It's much better to bring your own.

It's really easy to rent a car on the Big Island. There's a shuttle that will take you right from the Kona airport to the car rental lots. And in Hilo, you can return your car right at the airport and walk to the check-in counter.

I highly recommend booking a car through **Discount Hawaii Car Rentals**. They get the best rates for national car rental companies, including Dollar, Thrifty, Avis, Alamo, Budget, Enterprise, and Payless.

LATEST PRICES & AVAILABILITY

WHAT TO DO ON THE BIG ISLAND AT NIGHT

IF YOUR KIDS GO TO BED EARLY

After you put the kids to bed, send a parent to a nearby restaurant to grab dessert that you can enjoy on the lanai. A related idea is to create your own happy hour by making tropical cocktails. I've got some awesome **Hawaiian cocktail recipes**. If you are staying on the ground floor near the pool, you can enjoy a bit of late night pool time.

IF YOUR KIDS STAY UP LATE

For families that still have energy, you can do a few fun things after dinner. There are a few ice cream and shave ice places that stay open late (find ones near your hotel/condo). Many restaurants offer live music, which can be fun. You could also do an evening stroll on the beach or do some stargazing. Nighttime is also perfect for swimming with Manta Rays or doing a luau. And there's always pool time, just be sure to check when quiet hours begin.

WHERE TO FIND CHILDCARE

If you think you'll want a date night or want to do a tour/adventure that isn't kid-friendly, you'll probably want to hire a babysitter on the Big Island.

Here are a few places to find childcare during your vacation (although it's always best to book before your trip).

BIG ISLAND NANNIES ALOHA

MALIHINI KEIKI CARE

ALOHA NANNY

CAN I RENT BABY GEAR?

Absolutely and I highly recommend it. We rented an exersaucer when my oldest was a baby and it was SO helpful to have a safe place to put him while we got ready for the day. You can also rent playpens, sun tents, strollers, etc.

Here are the top places to rent baby gear on the Big Island:

ALOHA KONA KIDS ⊙   *TRAVELING BABY COMPANY* ⊙

BABY QUIP ⊙   *BABIES GETAWAY* ⊙

BABY'S AWAY ⊙

WHERE TO GET HAWAIIAN CLOTHING

If you are hoping to buy some cute Aloha wear for your luau, family photos, or just as a cool souvenir, there are plenty of places to find them on the Big Island.

Western Aloha is a Big Island brand that features paniolo (Hawaiian cowboy) motifs for a very unique Aloha shirt. They sell them at many Big Island boutiques.

If you're looking for high-end Aloha wear, head to Tori Richard at Kings Shops in Waikoloa. They have clothing for every member of your family and the quality is unsurpassed.

Costco in Kona is another place to find really good prices on high-quality Aloha wear. They typically always have mens shirts and it's hit/miss for women and children.

If you're looking for a budget option, Target in Kona or Hilo actually has a pretty decent selection for kids and adults. This is usually where we find the matching sets for babies and toddlers.

And don't count out thrift shops. If you want vintage Hawaiian clothing, you can find some cool items at great prices. Check out Kona Island Boutique and Thrift Store, KEC Full Circle Thrift Store, or Memory Lane Thrift Store.

WHERE TO FIND GROCERIES

The main grocery stores on the Big Island are Safeway, KTA Super Stores, and Sack N Save. If you'll be staying a week or longer, I definitely suggest heading to Costco in Kona to stock up. And Walmart has a pretty extensive grocery department. You can also find fresh produce at Big Island farmers markets that take place all across the island on different days of the week. There are a few natural food stores on the Big Island, as well.

HOW TO HANDLE DIRTY/SANDY LAUNDRY

We always put our sandy/wet clothing into plastic bags and then after they are somewhat dry, we shake them out to get all the sand off. You can hang them off the lanai to dry them out. Then, we put them in a packing cube with the rest of our dirty laundry. If you will be washing/drying in your condo, it's still important to get the sand off before you pop them in the washer.

Big Island with kids
TIPS & INFORMATION

BIG ISLAND WITH A BABY

I've got some general information about **Traveling to Hawaii with a Baby**, but I've also got some Big Island-specific advice I can share with you.

There's a flat, paved walking path at Old Kona Airport Beach that goes through some gardens and has pretty views. The beach also has cool tidepools that are fun to explore with babies and toddlers.

I also highly recommend buying an inflatable pool floatie that has a sun shade on it that you can use in your hotel pool or bring it to the beach. There's Onekahakaha Beach Park in Hilo or La'aloa Beach Park in Kailua-Kona that are perfect for babies and toddlers.

BIG ISLAND WITH TODDLERS

The Big Island is pretty fun with toddlers because they are able to do a little bit more than babies and you'll want to find things that will help get some wiggles out.

There are opportunities for toddlers and kids of all ages to swim with dolphins at the Hilton Waikoloa Village Resort. There's also the Pana'ewa Rainforest Zoo in Hilo that is perfect for little ones.

Something fun to do with older toddlers and preschoolers is the Atlantis Submarine in Kona. You can go underwater and see all kinds of incredible Hawaiian sea life and shipwrecks without getting wet.

BIG ISLAND WITH TEENS

The Big Island has some seriously cool places to go that will impress even the pickiest teen. Here are my top suggestions for teens on the Big Island:

INSTAGRAMMABLE SPOTS

For the teen who loves posting to Instagram or making TikToks, I'm happy to report that there are lots of Insta-worthy spots on the Big Island. For natural landscapes, head to the Waipio Valley Lookout for sweeping views of the coastline. Rainbow Falls and Akaka Falls are also perfect for the ultimate waterfall selfie. The Painted Church in Captain Cook is perfect for photos in a cute outfit. And Hawaii Volcanoes National Park has the opportunity to take photos of lava (or at least with a bunch of lava rock).

EPIC ADVENTURES

Teens who are at least 16 years old can drive their own ATV at Aloha Adventure Farms in Kona for the ultimate Big Island adventure. But, kids ages 5-15 can hop in a UTV and have a very similar experience. There's also snorkeling with Manta Rays at night that is a once-in-a-lifetime adventure. And if you're heading to the volcano, you can do an evening hike down to get close to the actual lava flow (as long as it's erupting).

ALI'I DRIVE

This is a great street in Kona where your teens can walk around and grab affordable food, Dole Whip, or shave ice. There are also lots of cute boutiques as well as souvenir shops, like the ABC store. And they can hang out on King Kam Beach, too.

IF YOU'RE HEADING TO THE
Big Island on a budget

CHEAP PLACES TO STAY

ROYAL KONA RESORT

The Royal Kona Resort is one of the closest hotels to Kona International Airport that could be considered "less expensive." They have everything you could ever need – tennis courts, a spa, a restaurant, pools, a saltwater lagoon, and much more! Plus, it's right on the highly-desirable location on Ali'i Drive.

PRICES & DETAILS ⊙

THE VOLCANO FOREST INN

The Volcano Forest Inn is a great choice for doing an overnight near Hawaii Volcanoes National Park. It's just an 8 minute walk to get into the park.

PRICES & DETAILS ⊙

HILO REEDS BAY HOTEL

Hilo Reeds Bay Hotel is located about 2 miles from the Hilo International Airport on Reeds Bay. There are three different kinds of rooms, each with their own pricing structure, and different rates for different numbers of occupants.

PRICES & DETAILS ⊙

10 THINGS THAT COST LESS THAN $10

1. THE BEACH
2. SHAVE ICE
3. COFFEE FARM TOURS
4. AKAKA FALLS STATE PARK
5. PANA'EWA RAINFOREST ZOO AND GARDENS
6. HAMAKUA MACADAMIA NUT FACTORY
7. MOKUPAPAPA DISCOVERY CENTER
8. RAINBOW FALLS
9. PUNALU'U BLACK SAND BEACH
10. KALOKO-HONOKŌHAU NATIONAL HISTORIC PARK

Hawaii PACKING LIST

Now that you know the types of activities you'll be doing on your Big Island vacation, it's time to start figuring out what to pack. I strongly recommend starting your packing list at least 2-3 weeks before your trip so you have enough time to order any items you don't have.

You'll want to have everyone try on their clothes before you pack them. You might be surprised that people have either outgrown their items or they are no longer comfortable. Same with shoes.

If you are staying somewhere with a washer/dryer, just pack for half your trip and do laundry. Otherwise, pack for your full trip plus an extra 2 outfits per person in case of spills/accidents.

WOMEN

- **DRESSES/SKIRTS:**
  Personally, I think wearing sundresses or skirts is the way to go in Hawaii because they keep you cool with the breeze. Plus, you can throw them on over swimsuits.

- **SHIRTS/TANKS:**
  Consider packing some that are a bit loose to help keep you cool.

- **SHORTS:**
  If you don't like to wear regular shorts, consider activewear short/skorts or pack extra skirts/dresses.

- **JACKET OR SWEATER:**
  It can get chilly in the evenings or early morning, especially during the winter months or when exploring Hawaii Volcanoes National Park.

- **SWIMSUIT:**
  You'll want at least 2 swimsuits so one can dry while you wear the other one. Plus, it's helpful to have a swimsuit coverup if you're staying at a resort.

- **"NICE" OUTFIT:**
  If you're doing a luau or going to a fancy restaurant, you'll want to pack either a dress or a blouse with slacks. This can also be your photo outfit.

- **FOOTWEAR:**
  You'll definitely want to bring a pair of sandals and flip flops. Depending on your activities, you might also need hiking shoes or water shoes.

- **UNDERWEAR:**
  Because it's warm in Hawaii, you might need to pack more bras than usual due to sweat. Personally, I think bralettes or wireless are most comfy in Hawaii, but bring whatever fits you best. Don't forget t-back or strapless bras, if needed.

MEN

- **T-SHIRTS/TANKS:**
  You might sweat through shirts quickly in Hawaii, so pack a few extras just in case.

- **POLO OR BUTTON DOWN SHIRT:**
  This is helpful if you attend a luau or go to a nice dinner. This can also be your photo outfit.

- **SLACKS OR KHAKIS:**
  These are what you'll wear with your polo or button down shirt.

- **SHORTS:**
  Bring along some lightweight shorts. The wick-free shorts are super helpful in Hawaii.

- **JACKET/SWEATSHIRT:**
  If you'll be doing a sunset boat ride, it can be helpful to have a jacket.

- **SWIMSUIT:**
  Bring at least 2 swimsuits so you can rotate them each day. You might also want a rashguard.

- **FOOTWEAR:**
  Definitely bring a pair of sandals and/or a nice pair of flip flops. Depending on your activities, you might also want hiking shoes or water shoes.

- **UNDERWEAR:**
  Bring at least one for every day of your trip (and more if you plan on swimming a lot/changing your clothes frequently).

KIDS

- **T-SHIRTS/TANKS:**
  We usually bring enough for our trip plus an extra 3-4 shirts per kid in case of food spills or something.

- **SHORTS:**
  Definitely bring at least enough shorts for every day of your trip.

- **"NICE" OUTFIT:**
  Pack something they can wear to the luau or out to dinner, or plan on buying some cute Aloha wear when you get to the Big Island. This can also be your photo outfit.

- **JACKET/SWEATSHIRT:**
  This can be nice if you end up going for a beachwalk in the early morning because they wake up at the crack of dawn.

- **SWIMSUIT AND RASHGUARD:**
  Pack at least 2 swimsuits and rashguards per kid. If they won't wear a damp/cold swimsuit, pack 3.

- **FOOTWEAR:**
  Kids can basically just wear sandals the whole time. Although they might need closed toe shoes for activities. Plus, it's nice to have water shoes if they might explore tidepools.

CARRY ON ITEMS

Something a lot of families don't spend too much time thinking about is their bag for the airplane. I actually have a big list of airplane packing essentials, but here are the highlights.

- **ELECTRONICS:**
  Make sure to pack your tablets, camera, laptop, devices, plus any charging cables you might need during the flight.

- **SNACKS:**
  Trust me, you'll want to bring about twice as many snacks as you think you'll need. It will stave off crankiness.

- **WATER BOTTLE:**
  You can fill it up with water at the airport or pour the complimentary airplane drinks into it to minimize kid spills.

- **SWEATER:**
  Sometimes the airplanes will blow cold air the entire trip and many don't offer blankets.

- **LYSOL WIPES:**
  We wipe down anything our kids might touch.

- **DIAPERS/PULL-UPS:**
  Definitely bring a few more than you expect. And it's handy to pack them in a pull out bag to take to the lavatory.

TOILETRIES

- **REEF SAFE SUNSCREEN:**
  It's the only sunscreen allowed in Hawaii.

- **AFTER SUN LOTION:**
  We really like Maui Vera because it has a nice cooling effect.

- **NEOSPORIN:**
  It's always helpful to pack this when traveling with kids.

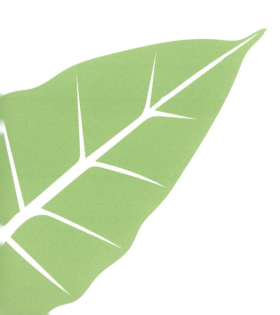

PRINTABLE PACKING LIST

WOMEN

- [ ] DRESSES/SKIRTS
- [ ] SHIRTS/TANKS
- [ ] SHORTS
- [ ] JACKET OR SWEATER
- [ ] SWIMSUIT
- [ ] "NICE" OUTFIT
- [ ] FOOTWEAR
- [ ] UNDERWEAR
- [ ] _____
- [ ] _____
- [ ] _____
- [ ] _____

MEN

- [ ] T-SHIRTS/TANKS
- [ ] POLO OR BUTTON DOWN SHIRT
- [ ] SLACKS OR KHAKIS
- [ ] SHORTS
- [ ] JACKET/SWEATSHIRT
- [ ] SWIMSUIT
- [ ] FOOTWEAR
- [ ] UNDERWEAR
- [ ] _____
- [ ] _____
- [ ] _____
- [ ] _____

KIDS

- [ ] T-SHIRTS/TANKS
- [ ] SHORTS
- [ ] "NICE" OUTFIT
- [ ] JACKET/SWEATSHIRT
- [ ] SWIMSUIT AND RASHGUARD
- [ ] FOOTWEAR
- [ ] _____
- [ ] _____
- [ ] _____
- [ ] _____

CARRY ON

- [ ] ELECTRONICS
- [ ] SNACKS
- [ ] WATER BOTTLE
- [ ] SWEATER
- [ ] LYSOL WIPES
- [ ] DIAPERS/PULL-UPS
- [ ] _____
- [ ] _____
- [ ] _____
- [ ] _____
- [ ] _____

TOILETRIES

- [ ] REEF SAFE SUNSCREEN
- [ ] AFTER SUN LOTION
- [ ] NEOSPORIN
- [ ] _____
- [ ] _____
- [ ] _____
- [ ] _____
- [ ] _____

Activities PACKING LIST

Now that you have a general Big Island packing list, I'm breaking down the items you'll need for some of the top activities/adventures.

BEACH DAY

The Big Island has some of the prettiest beaches that are awesome for kids. If you are heading to the Big Island with a baby, I've got a complete list of my Beach Packing Essentials for Babies. Otherwise, these are the top 3 things to bring.

- **WATERPROOF BEACH BAG:**
  Sometimes the sand is damp or your kids dump water on your bag, so it's really helpful to bring one that is waterproof. I also add in wet/dry bags for swimsuits and other things I want to keep separate from the rest of my bag.

- **MICROFIBER TOWEL:**
  Bringing regular beach towels can take up SO much space. The little microfiber towels are so much easier. Plus, some are even sandproof.

- **BABY POWDER:**
  This is a total island hack for easily getting sand off of feet and legs before hopping in the car. Sprinkle it anywhere you have sand and then dust off with a towel.

SNORKELING TRIP

One of the most popular Big Island excursions is doing a snorkeling boat tour. There are tons to choose from and it really helps if you pack the right items to ensure a safe and fun trip.

- **SPF CLOTHING:**
  You'll be out in the elements for at least a half-day, so you'll want to make sure to protect your skin. Plus, it can get really windy and the salt spray can dry your skin out. Wearing long sleeve SPF shirts or jackets can really minimize that.

- **REEF SAFE SUNSCREEN:**
  You'll definitely want to wear sunscreen and re-apply it often.

- **NAUSEA MEDICINE:**
  Even if you don't normally get motion sickness, it's helpful to have something on hand in case the water is extra choppy.

HIKING DAY

The Big Island is known for its epic hiking trails. Some are kid-friendly and some are for much more experienced hikers. I've got a big list of hiking essentials, but here are my top things to pack.

- **BUG REPELLENT:**
  A lot of Big Island hikes are in the jungle and that can get really buggy. Same goes for the ones near water. Put on some bug repellent before your hike and then re-apply on the way back.

- **CLOSED TOE SHOES/SANDALS:**
  While it may seem tempting to hike in flip flops, it can be really dangerous and you might injure yourself. I recommend wearing old shoes or dark shoes because Big Island's red dirt will stain.

- **SUN HAT:**
  Even if you think you'll be in the shade, you might be surprised just how sunny some of these hiking trails can be. Throw some in your bag so you're prepared.

LUAU

Another popular thing to do on the Big Island is attend a Hawaiian luau. These can be a lot of fun and it's usually a bit expensive, so you'll want to make the most out of it.

- **FLAT SHOES/SANDALS:**
  Many luaus take place on grass and if you wear heels, you might get stuck if the grass is mushy. Much better to wear flats or wedges (if you want some height).

- **STROLLER/BABY CARRIER:**
  If you have a baby or toddler, chances are they will get sleepy sometime between dinner and the show. It's nice to let them fall asleep in either a stroller or a baby carrier so you can still enjoy the luau. Win win!

- **VIDEO CAMERA OR GIMBAL:**
  Because there are so many fun luau activities, it can be really nice to capture them on video. I usually bring my Osmo Pocket mini video camera but you can also get a gimbal for your phone if you want to take your video skills to the next level. Both are super easy to use and you'll capture the cutest memories with your kids.

Hawaii WORDS TO KNOW

It's always helpful to know a few local words when you travel. Even though Hawaii is part of the United States, you'll see and hear Hawaiian words all the time. These are the top ones I think every family should know before their trip.

ALOHA *(ah-LOW-hah)*

Most people know that the word Aloha means hello, but it also means goodbye and love. It's the most popular greeting in Hawaii.

MAHALO *(mah-HALL-oh)*

This means thank you and you should use it anytime someone does anything for you. It's always better to be polite!

KEIKI *(KAY-kee)*

This is the Hawaiian word for kids. A kids menu at restaurants is called the keiki menu and you'll see kids prices at tourist attractions and tours called keiki prices.

KAMA'AINA *(KAH-ma-EYE-nah)*

This is the term for people who live in Hawaii and have Hawaii ID. You'll see Kama'aina rates listed everywhere because residents usually get a discount.

OHANA *(oh-HA-nah)*

If you watched *Lilo & Stitch*, you know Ohana means family! Sometimes you'll see the price for an Ohana meal, and that means it's enough to share with your family.

KU'UIPO *(koo-ooh-EE-poh)*

This is the Hawaiian term for sweetheart. You'll also see this printed on jewelry.

MAUKA *(MAOW-kah)*

When people give directions, they often say Mauka if they mean toward the mountain.

MA KAI *(mah-KAI)*

This means toward the ocean, and is a common term when giving directions.

KOKUA *(koh-KOO-ah)*

You'll see trash cans that say Please Kokua and that simply means "please help" by throwing away your trash.

A HUI HOU *(ah-HOO-ee-HOE)*

This is the Hawaiian term for "until next time" and you'll hear it at the end of luaus, the airplane safety video, and just about everywhere.

HAWAII PRINTABLES & CRAFTS *for Kids*

PRINTABLES

Whether you are homeschooling, worldschooling, or just want to keep your kids busy for a few minutes, it can be nice to have some Hawaii-themed printables. These are great for the plane ride or to get your kids extra excited for the trip.

AT THE BEACH WORKSHEETS

MERMAID ACTIVITY PACK

SEA ANIMAL WORKSHEETS & COLORING PAGES

SEA LIFE COLOR BY NUMBER PRINTABLE

SEA TURTLE ACTIVITY PACK

GECKO ACTIVITY PACK

UNDER THE SEA MEMORY MATCHING GAME

HAWAII WORD SEARCH AND WORD SCRAMBLES

HAWAII COLORING SHEETS & ACTIVITY PAGES

CRAFTS

Another fun thing to do before or after your trip to Hawaii are crafts! These are some of our favorite, fairly easy Hawaii crafts for kids.

PLUMERIA PAPER FLOWERS

PAPER WHALES

ORIGAMI SHARKS

MACRAME RAINBOW WALL HANGING

HAWAIIAN PAPER LEI

DISNEY MOANA PAPER DOLL

PINEAPPLE CORK STAMPING

OCEAN ANIMAL SUNCATCHERS

VOLCANO EXPERIMENTS

NOTES:

NOTES:

NOTES:

NOTES:

NOTES:

NOTES:

NOTES:

NOTES:

NOTES:

NOTES:

NOTES:

NOTES:

NOTES:

NOTES:

NOTES:

NOTES:

NOTES:

NOTES:

NOTES:

NOTES:

NOTES:

NOTES:

NOTES:

NOTES:

NOTES:

NOTES:

NOTES:

NOTES:

NOTES:

NOTES:

NOTES:

Made in United States
Troutdale, OR
12/23/2023

16392647R00045